THE THING IN THE
GAP-STONE STILE

The Thing in the Gap-stone Stile

Alice Oswald

Oxford   New York
OXFORD UNIVERSITY PRESS
1996

Oxford University Press, Walton Street, Oxford OX2 6DP

Oxford New York
Athens Auckland Bangkok Bombay
Calcutta Cape Town Dar es Salaam Delhi
Florence Hong Kong Istanbul Karachi
Kuala Lumpur Madras Madrid Melbourne
Mexico City Nairobi Paris Singapore
Taipei Tokyo Toronto
and associated companies in
Berlin Ibadan

Oxford is a trade mark of Oxford University Press

First published in Oxford Poets
as an Oxford University Press paperback 1996

British Library Cataloguing in Publication Data
Data available

Library of Congress Cataloging in Publication Data
Oswald, Alice, 1966–
The thing in the Gap-stone stile / Alice Oswald.
I. Title.
PS3565.S96M46   1996   811'.54—dc20   95-23754
ISBN 0-19-282513-5

1 3 5 7 9 10 8 6 4 2

Typeset by Rowland Phototypesetting Limited
Printed in Hong Kong

ACKNOWLEDGEMENTS

Poems from this collection first appeared in: *Planet* (*The Welsh Internationalist*), *London Magazine, New Statesman, Spectator, The Forward Book of Poetry 1993,* and in *Anvil New Poets 2,* edited by Carol Ann Duffy (1995).

A collection of twenty poems was given an Eric Gregory Award in 1994.

CONTENTS

PRUNING IN FROST

Last night, without a sound,
a ghost of a world lay down on a world,

trees like dream-wrecks
coralled with increments of frost.

Found crevices
and wound and wound
the clock-spring cobwebs.

All life's ribbon frozen mid-fling.

Oh I am
stone thumbs,
feet of glass.

Work knocks in me the winter's nail.

I can imagine
Pain, turned heron,
could fly off slowly in a creak of wings.

And I'd be staring, like one of those
cold-holy and granite kings,
getting carved into this effigy of orchard.

A GREYHOUND IN THE EVENING AFTER A LONG DAY OF RAIN

Two black critical matching crows,
calling a ricochet, eating its answer,

dipped
    home

and a minute later
the ground was a wave and the sky wouldn't float.

*

With a task and a rake,
with a clay-slow boot and a yellow mack,
I bolted for shelter under the black strake dripping of timber,

summer of rain, summer of green rain
coming everywhere all day down
through a hole in my foot.

*

Listen Listen Listen Listen

*

They are returning to the rain's den,
the grey folk, rolling up their veils,
taking the steel taps out of their tips and heels.

Grass lifts, hedge breathes,
rose shakes its hair,
birds bring out all their washed songs,
puddles like long knives flash on the roads.

*

And evening is come with a late sun unloading a silence,
tiny begin-agains dancing on the night's edge.

But what I want to know is
whose is the great grey wicker-limber hound,
like a stepping on coal, going softly away . . .

THE GLASS HOUSE

The glass house is a hole in the rain,
the sun's chapel,
a bell for the wind.

Cucumbers, full of themselves,
the long green lungs of that still air,

image the fruits of staying put,
like water-beetles in woodland puddles
and hoofprints.

And I
am a hole in the glass house,
taking my time between the rows.

The leaves, the yellow blooms, the pots
vanish through a loop of thoughts.

Then far off
comes the cluck-sound of this green can
dipping and spilling . . .
and dipping again.

MY NEIGHBOUR, MRS KERSEY

That noise, Mrs Kersey—were you listening?
A tin roof warping and booming . . .

Our sitting rooms connect like shears
into the screw-pin of our fires.

We share a bird's nest in a common chimney.
If I'm right, you breathe, Mrs Kersey,

close as a dream-self on the other side.
This wall, if you just rubbed an eyelid,

is a bricked-up looking glass.
And wind across that roof's a loss

of difference to whatever's moving
privately through our heads this evening.

Like the clicking of my jaw,
the tic-tac of your solitaire.

SLEEP

Now our close heads, like under a gravestone,
are intact and locked. We turn,
in the thrift of sleep, each to his own;

negotiate, in the same place,
one feat—the sucking and blowing
eight hours of air at a steady pace.

Imagine—you who can leap a gate
feet together with one hand on the bar
and swing to a halt for a second as you float . . .

in many kinds, in cobwebs, under wings,
on paws, in shells, the breathing enters you
into a unity of drowsing things;

and when I wake, the only sound's a sequel
of absurd tasks—this heaviness of air
and how you roll it uphill and downhill.

POEM

You ask me why did I lie down
and when and never rose again.

I of the bluebells
layed on a succulent mattress, frown.

And ask me when shall I get up
and blink and see my friends again.

I run my fingers round my lip,
transmuted to a bluebell cup.

A spider swings from bloom to bloom.
A fungus detonates and slowly
leaf contusions rot to rheum.

And every which way my fly-about eyes
catch this and that and my half-replies,
seduced by visions, vaporise.

It's when you've gone,
(the quiet woods creaking after rain),
my voice, a pollen dust, puffs out
the reason I remain:

here I give up the difficult dice
of friendship and I crook my knees
into a zed beneath the trees.
I watch in miniature of man
such intricate affairs as these,
these bluebells tussling for the sun.

A WOOD COMING INTO LEAF

From the first to the second

Warily, from the tip to the palm

Third leaf (the blackthorn done)

From the fourth to the fifth and
(Larix, Castanea, Fraxinus, Tilia)

Thaw taps, groping in stumps,
frost like an adder easing away

The sixth to the seventh (plums conceive
a knobble in a stone within a blossom)

Ushers the next by the thumbs to the next . . .

A thirty-first, a thirty-second

A greenwood through a blackwood
passes (like the moon's halves
meet and go behind themselves)

And you and I, quarter-alight, our boots in shadow

Birch, oak, rowan, ash
chinese-whispering the change.

SONNET

When I sit up this late, breathing like so
into the growing soap-ball of my silence,
I just can't think and I don't want to know
whether I've lost my heart to my resilience;
not care, not speak—the clock, the book, the chair
and this one self, beyond sufficiency,
gone like an oyster to the ocean's floor
to make of love the pearl's cold quality . . .
I chose to think of you but I can't say
whether it's peace or makeshift that I live
in this last zero of the millionth day
which ends like this, just breathing to survive.
And I don't know and so I haven't said
whether it's you or nothing in my head.

SONNET

I can't sleep in case a few things you said
no longer apply. The matter's endless,
but definitions alter what's ahead
and you and words are like a hare and tortoise.
Aaaagh there's no description—each a fractal
sectioned by silences, we have our own
skins to feel through and fall back through—awful
to make so much of something so unknown.
But even I—some shower-swift commitments
are all you'll get; I mustn't gauge or give
more than I take—which is a way to balance
between misprision and belief in love
both true and false, because I'm only just
short of a word to be the first to trust.

since love is round and man misshapen
it may not always accord and if I
and I do furiously reprove myself
hackle up and without impulse cry
or if after if I hum for hours
all cold and odd and feign mad
and vanish with my jacket on my head
and your calm hands just lift and let it by . . .
I say a miracle a notion at risk
and grown of and aloof to faults and a
terrible demand is love but if you ask
something of refund on your gentleness
and in good time take secretly
another girl and say so guiltily . . .
then leave me I haven't such forgiveness . . .

EPITAPH

She was like . . .

what was it I feared about a thrown black ball
without a sound, per second per second,
hypercatalectically on the hesitation of its fall
making for its own shape and going through it?

I can still see it,
everybody running up the lawn
yelling 'THUNDER' as it whispers down . . .

and that hysterical dog
at the end of the back lane
where the old buses were
between the tin sheds and the flowering thorn

trotting to and fro, just
trotting to and fro until we'd gone . . .

between the curtains as they shut,
one of my wild selves
moving to me from beyond the glass . . .

she was like that.

APRIL

The sheer grip and the push of it—growth gets
a footledge in the loosest stems, it takes
the litterings of weeds and clocks them round;
your eyeballs bud and alter and you can't
step twice in the same foot—I know a road,
the curve throws it one way and another;
somebody slipped the gears and bucketed slowly
into the hawthorns and his car took root
and in its bonnet now, amazing flowers
appear and fade and quiddify the month;
and us on bicycles—it was so fast
wheeling and turning we were lifted falling,
our blue-sky jackets filling up like vowels . . .
and now we float in the fair blow of springtime,
kingfishers, each astonishing the other
to be a feathered nerve, to take the crack
between the river's excess and the sun's.

WOMAN IN A MUSTARD FIELD

From love to light my element
was altered when I fled
out of your house to meet the space
that blows about my head.

The sun was rude and sensible,
the rivers ran for hours
and whoops I found a mustard field
exploding into flowers;

and I slowly came to sense again
the thousand forms that move
all summer through a living world
that grows without your love.

BIKE RIDE ON A ROMAN ROAD

This Roman road—eye's axis
over the earth's rococo curve—
is a road's road to ride in a dream.

I am bound to a star,
my own feet shoving me swiftly.

Everything turns but the North is the same.

Foot Foot, under the neck-high bracken
a little random man, with his head in a bad
controversy of midges,
flickers away singing Damn Damn

and the line he runs is serpentine,
everything happens at sixes and sevens,
the jump and the ditch and the crooked stile . . .

and my two eyes are floating in the fields,
my mouth is on a branch, my hair
is miles behind me making tributaries
and I have had my heart distracted out of me,
my skin is blowing slowly about without me

and now I have no hands and now I have no feet.

This is the road itself
riding a bone bicycle through my head.

THE MOON ADDRESSES HER REFLECTION

In this floating world, in this floating world,
you are a kind of nothingness and far less fine than a tiger
and I inhabit one of the jagged disassembled islands.

If you so wish, you can find me
up a high rock in the wind,
discreet of foot, claws in a glove, just
rubbing my yew-burr knees.

I have a moon's task—staring at seas.

Women and men, like dolphins,
fluke and sound, pushing their lives above the waves.

But you and I, who know each other's nothingness,
are lonely, like the blues beyond
(the sky-ghost turning its mirrors under the sky-ghost).

And with huge care, closer and closer,
if we so wish we could
deliberately condense our lightness
into the weights and disciplines of love.

Or you can leave me,
powerful on my rock
and as you go, reduce me to a moon.

SEA SONNET

Green, grey and yellow, the sea and the weather
instantiate each other and the spectrum
turns in it like a perishable creature.
The sea is old but the blue sea is sudden.

The wind japans the surface. Like a flower,
each point of contact biggens and is gone.
And when it rains the senses fold in four.
No sky, no sea—the whiteness is all one.

So I have made a little moon-like hole
with a thumbnail and through a blade of grass
I watch the weather make the sea my soul,
which is a space performed on by a space;

and when it rains, the very integer
and shape of water disappears in water.

SEA SONNET

The sea is made of ponds—a cairn of rain.
It has an island flirting up and down
like a blue hat. A boat goes in between.

Is made of rills and springs—each waternode
a tiny subjectivity, the tide
coordinates their ends, the sea is made.

The sea crosses the sea, the sea has hooves;
the powers of rivers and the weir's curves
are moving in the wind-bent acts of waves.

And then the softer waters of the wells
and soakaways—hypostases of holes,
which swallow up and sink for seven miles;

and then the boat arriving on the island
and nothing but the sea-like sea beyond.

SEA SONNET

A field, a sea-flower, three stones, a stile.
Not one thing close to another
throughout air. The cliff's uplifted lawns.
You and I walk light as wicker in virtual contact.

Prepositions lie exposed. All along
the swimmer is deeper than the water.
I have looked under the wave,
I saw your body floating on the darkness.

Oh time and water cannot touch.
Not touch. Only a blob far out,
your singularity and the sea's
inalienable currents flow at angles . . .

and if I love you this is incidental
as on the sand one blue towel, one white towel.

ESTUARY SONNET

As much as I walk by and see the water
up to the second line, I skim a slate
and in the time it sinks my feet are wet
and there are huge boats lifting in the harbour.

And then as far as I have time to wander,
I wander back and there's a heron's foot
lofting the water which is now a mud-flat
and some old shipwreck gnawn to its vertebrae.

Touch me the moment where these worlds collide,
the river's cord unravelled by the tide . . .

and I will show you nothing—neither high
nor low nor salt nor fresh—only the skill
of tiny creatures like the human eye
to live by water, which is never still.

I BICYCLED PAST A SHIP

Last night I saw the watermoon
in such a frantic dance
that I could feel the drift of it
in my own feet and hands.

Woodsmoke moving to the wind
or in a secret place
a woman dancing on her own
were less engrossed than this.

What was it with the moon and moon,
one inarticulate the other dumb,
each on edge and staring round
in the same holy vaccuum?

I saw them shed the world away
of every shape but one
and then a ship came sliding by
between the moon and moon.

CONDE ARNALDOS

It was the morning of San Juan.
The blue sea was coming in.
Conde Arnaldos ran and ran.
The sea was brushing on the sand.

He had his falcon on his hand.
He saw the boat upon the waters.
When he was hunting for small creatures,
the boat was sailing for the land.

And all the sails were made of shadows,
the yellow mast was made of willows
and in the shadows was a sailor
who sang a song to a guitar.

'What is your song?' said Conde Arnaldos.
The song was magic I am sure.
It brought the fishes to the surface,
it made the seagulls fly in circles.

'What is your song?' said Conde Arnaldos
and the sailor said 'Por Dios—
I will sing my song but only
if you will sail away with me.'

(*based on an anonymous Spanish ballad*)

THE PILCHARD-CURING SONG

(adapted from the Cornish of John Boson)

I sing of pilchards, caught on a rod
in the Bay of the Grey Rock in the wood.
'Tithe! Tithe!' Over the sea
the boats come home to a cry on the quay;
every big woman, with her bum upwards,
swinging away with a creel of pilchards.
Back at home, it's a day's turn
crying 'Holan moy for my hern hern!'
and in a month they'll be salted dry;
then break them up and pull them away
and a dirty girl can give them a wash
till her hands come up as clean as the fish.
Put them bright in barrels, head to tail.
Your pilchard is a profitable sale.
Then look for a log of thirteen feet
and a heap of stones five hundredweight
and keep an eye on the slow continual
drip-drop of oil from the barrel.
This is the true way. This is your standard
top quality market pilchard.
Year upon year, the boats'll take
loads of them from the Gwavas Lake
and a north-east wind'll blow them far
to where the well-heeled foreigners are
and everywhere it's the same trouble:
more of poor people, less of rich people.

PRIVET PROPERTY

Oh Mrs Kersey, my hedge is your hedge.
And you have it clipped just so far
and I have it hippy just so far . . .

The long and the short of it is
our hedge has a ledge.

I am tall, you are small.
That sky is MY sky—

but you're welcome to wave things
as far as the line that isn't mine
over the privet, if you can't see above it.

(We'd be remote
except your stockings float between,
without their owner being seen.)

BALLAD OF A SHADOW

Take from me my voice and I shall voiceless go
to find you; take from me my face,
I'll treck the hills invisibly,
my strength, and I shall run but keep no pace.

Even in cities, take the sense with which I reason
and I shall seek, but close it in your heart,
keep this and forget this
and this, when we're apart,

will be the shadow game of love.
And I shall love in secret
and I shall love in crowds
and love in darkness, in the quiet

outlet of shadows, and in cities
as a ghost walking unnoticed,
and love with books, using their pages like a wind,
not reading, and with people, latticed

by words but through the lattice loving.
And when at last my love is understood,
with you I shall not love but breathe
and turn by breathing into flesh and blood.

WEDDING

From time to time our love is like a sail
and when the sail begins to alternate
from tack to tack, it's like a swallowtail
and when the swallow flies it's like a coat;
and if the coat is yours, it has a tear
like a wide mouth and when the mouth begins
to draw the wind, it's like a trumpeter
and when the trumpet blows, it blows like millions . . .
and this, my love, when millions come and go
beyond the need of us, is like a trick;
and when the trick begins, it's like a toe
tip-toeing on a rope, which is like luck;
and when the luck begins, it's like a wedding,
which is like love, which is like everything.

OTTER OUT AND IN

Collision of opposites which pulls the river
plucks the otter through an aperture
and lays and breeds the river, high and low,
through Dipper Mill in her absorbing beauty;

and brings us running from the field
and throws and cleaves us into shadows
arm in arm and apart upon the water;
and flexes the otter in and out the water.

The whole river transforms upon an otter.
Now and gone, sometimes we see him
swimming above the fish—half-of-the-air,
half-of-the-darkness—when he dives,

a duck-flip into darkness, creep
close to the edge and closer. There are times
when water's attentiveness
is tight enough to walk on

and we came so strangely
out of the darkness to this world
of watersounds colliding slowly,
out and in and disappear in darkness . . .

OWL VILLAGE

There is a place between an owl
and a tall crowd of equal lines,
a wood of wishbone trees.

Half air, half village,
it murmurs, like the mind upon the brain

and people with carrier bags
walking symmetrically between their hands,
they live like that in a poise of pressures.

The neighbours regard each oddity until it goes . . .

*

At eight o'clock, I opened the window to the woods
and an owl about the size of a vicar
tumbled across in a boned gown

and then a fleet of owls, throwing the hoot between them,
owls with two faces singing Ave and Ouch Ave and Ouch . . .

*

and you and I—comprehension burst its container
twice, in that the ear
extends through us beyond the ear—

we grew aware of the villagers
in bird clothes afloat among the trees
singing Libera me Domine Deo

and the disseverence of ourselves,
as if we stood, one dead, the other alone.

IF STONES COULD FLY

Having watched a spider closely,
I find there is a stone in it,
cleverly lifted and set rolling,
like a kite manoeuvres a man.

Or an orbit, approaching its pole
by compensatory poise and pull,
corybantic and following threads
and doing shrift of spooling and crawling,

visions of unspannable air
spin her, making the silk a wheel
that struts and hubs and rims a gap
between a rafter and a sack.

But it's a stone's life—this needing a web—
and what'd fly if it were made
is tethered to a dropping thing
which halves the loveliness of floating.

THE THING IN THE GAP-STONE STILE

I took the giant's walk on top of world,
peak-striding, each step a viaduct.

I dropped hankies, cut from a cloth of hills,
and beat gold under fields
for the sun to pick out a patch.

I never absolutely told
the curl-horned cows to line up their gaze.
But it happened, so I let it be.

And Annual Meadow Grass, quite of her own accord,
between the dry-stone spread out emerald.

(I was delighted by her initiative
and praised the dry-stone for being contrary.)

What I did do (I am a gap)
was lean these elbows on a wall
and sat on my hunkers pervading the boulders.

My pose became the pass across two kingdoms,
before behind antiphonal, my cavity the chord.

And I certainly intended
anyone to be almost
abstracted on a gap-stone between fields.

WHEN A STONE WAS WRECKING
HIS COUNTRY

When a man went to fight a stone,
he clenched his knuckle-stones, he lifted his foot-stones,
he upheld himself like the last megalith,
he kissed his lady like a white abandonable sea-pebble,
he felt as justified as a set slate.

He saw the sky like an open flint
and the starlings shaken and fallen about like gravel.
He wanted to go carefully like making a wall.
He went as far as meteorites disappear
into the holes and shadows of the universe like a curious
        pumice;

went among tree boughs like the dark detail of marble,
went among animals like various amethysts
and men of rock and flowers extempore as lava
and came to confusion like a heap of shale.
He came to despair like moisture coming up through chalk.

He had to oppose everything, he had to grind away
at his own tooth-stones, saying:
'if I could sift the silicate from these bones,
if this complexion of feldspar,
if this ego-dragon spiralling like a fossil . . .'

but he couldn't rest like a little grit under an eyelid
till his head like some god-in-a-boulder
rolled from its purpose and came down among stone-kind.

MOUNTAINS

Something is in the line and air along edges,
which is in woods when the leaf changes
and in the leaf-pattern's gives and gauges,
the water's tension upon ledges.
Something is taken up with entrances,
which turns the issue under bridges.
The moon is between places.
An outlet fills the space between two horses.

Look through a holey stone. Now put it down.
Something is twice as different. Something gone
accumulates a queerness. Be alone.
Something is side by side with anyone.

And certain evenings, something in the balance
falls to the dewpoint where our minds condense
and then inslides itself between moments
and spills the heart from its circumference;
and this is when the moon matchlessly opens
and you can feel by instinct in the distance
the bigger mountains hidden by the mountains,
like intentions among suggestions.

GARDENERS AT THE RESURRECTION

Damp of sleeve, working inattentively,
naming insects, gauging the sky,

considering the life
and knocking the mud off,

in a through place of rooks and wagtails
and cloud-shadows like slow pterodactyls,

they bent low, they lamented the weather;
the sun picked and chose like a fault-finder

and it rained on the kale pots
and the wind belaboured the cabbage nets . . .

they with round backs
carried the hours like peat sacks,

dug perfect cubes,
despised office jobs

and tossed the rotten one
and took the barrows in

and saw two men talking intently
and whistled softly and went on steadily.

THE GARDENERS IN THE SHED

Tense your lungs against the slick
breathed out of petrol kegs.

The shed's a wooden card-house,
likely to flap over in a wind.

Light-sheets glide under the door.
The windows are webbed cloudy.

Looped ropes like tropical snakes
poise on a peg, self-belted in their tails.

And we gardeners stare at our boots
and tunes of clinking spades begin and stop.

He came in with a beautiful
caterpillar twisting in a jar.

We watched it twisting and twisting.
Ah but his photographs—we flew,

holding them so gently,
through better worlds:

beaches, boats, a picnic,
ladies in a hat's eclipse . . .

and to think of them still rolling beneath us,
naming odd plants in Australia.

THE APPLE SHED

It suddenly thunders and the blue cloud
cracks O run for the sheds
in the clap of time . . .

when it flashes and flashes and the tin sky flickers in the
        thick of echoes,
clear the benches, space the apples,
think of the ten quiet trees with their nerves in the air.

The eye of the storm is my own fear . . .

I wouldn't risk a finger out of doors,
not even for a glancing look
to fetch the key that hangs on the nail
to cross the courtyard to the loo and back

twenty paces under a moving cloudslip . . .

        halfway, caught running in a light from heaven,
        I saw myself struck stiff, but it was just
        the grandeur of thunder, the sheer
        impact of the thought that knocked me blind

and now the comfortable dropping sound
of rain as heavy as a shower of apples:

Ribston Pippin, Cox's Orange,
Woolbrook Russet, Sturmer Pippin,
Bramley, Crispin, Margil, Spartan,
Beauty of Bath and Merton Beauty . . .

Put them bright in rows. Tell me
what have our souls been growing all these years
of time taken and rendered back as apples?

THE MELON GROWER

She concerned him,
but the connection had come loose.
They made shift with tiffs and silence.

He sowed a melon seed.
He whistled in the greenhouse.
She threw a slipper at him

and something jostled in the loam
as if himself had been layed blind.
She misperceived him. It rained.

The melon got eight leaves, it lolled.
She banged the plates.
He considered his fretful webby hands.

'If I can sex' he said 'the flowers,
very gently I'll touch their parts
with a pollen brush made of rabbit hairs.'

The carpels swelled. He had to prop them on pots.
She wanted the house repainting.
He was out the back watering.

He went to church, he sang 'O Lord how long shall the
        wicked . . . ?'
He prayed, with his thumbs on his eyes.
His head, like a melon, pressured his fingers.

The shoots lengthened
and summer mornings came with giant shadows
and arcs as in the interim of a resurrection.

She stayed in bed, she was coughing.
He led the side-shoots along the wires.
She threw the entire tea-trolley downstairs.

And when the milk was off
and when his car had two flat tyres
and when his daughter left saying she'd had enough,

he was up a ladder hanging soft nets from the beam
to stop the fruit so labouring the stem.
The four globes grew big at ease

and a melony smell filled the whole place
and he caught her once, confused in the greenhouse,
looking for binder-twine. Or so she says.

PRAYER

Here I work in the hollow of God's hand
with Time bent round into my reach. I touch
the circle of the earth, I throw and catch
the sun and moon by turns into my mind.
I sense the length of it from end to end,
I sway me gently in my flesh and each
point of the process changes as I watch;
the flowers come, the rain follows the wind.

And all I ask is this—and you can see
how far the soul, when it goes under flesh,
is not a soul, is small and creaturish—
that every day the sun comes silently
to set my hands to work and that the moon
turns and returns to meet me when it's done.

THE THREE WISE MEN OF GOTHAM
WHO SET OUT TO CATCH THE MOON
IN A NET

INTRODUCTION

In the thirteenth century, the people of Gotham were expecting a visit from King John. This would have been expensive (it involved collection of taxes and even the laying of a road to welcome him), so they decided to put him off by pretending to be mad. They began drowning eels, fishing for the moon, getting dressed by jumping out of trees into trousers; they even built a wall around a thicket to stop a cuckoo escaping. This, they said, would prolong the spring. King John avoided the town.

This poem describes their journey to catch the moon. It includes a reference to Thomas Love Peacock's song:

> Seamen three! What men be ye?
> Gotham's three wise men we be . . .
> Who art thou, so fast adrift?
> I am he they call Old Care . . .

and also to the legend of seven fishermen who came home in tears because one of their company had drowned; in fact they had simply miscalculated: each man was counting the six people he could see, and forgetting himself.

It was a monday night. The moon was up
and throwing golden elvers on the water.
Long bows of wind were swerving on the quay.
A man came down, whose purpose was to catch
the watermoon—whatever flower or fish
the light took shape as, shifting and dividing.
He was a butcher. He came shouting by
as if the art of thinking were a pommel
to pound the world into conformity;
'The moon,' he said, 'in that it is a magnet,
moves independently and has a soul,
the motor principle of which . . .' the wind
had found a cave of whispers in his coat
and in a line of sailing boats a tune
to jingle on the halyards; tiny waves
were running in the puddles . . . 'O the moon—
how many miles' he said 'to catch a moon?'

He had two friends—a baker and a maker
of candlesticks—who didn't know the answer.
The one had been on nights, laying the loaves
in rows on stainless trays, when he looked up
and saw this woman floating at the window:
'Ave Maria the moon is full of grace . . .'
He dropped his knife. He switched the ovens off
and ran to meet the butcher in the harbour
just as the other, in his dark workshop
where he was turning woodblocks into spirals
to make a candlestick, the loveliness
and quiet of moonlight drew him to the door;
and he was blind—a single iron wire
ran through his eyelids, stitching them together—
but even so, the moon enchanted him
to move by touch and spaces to the harbour.

'Who's there?' 'Who's with you?' 'No one' 'just the moon'
'Can I come with you?' 'I was half asleep'
'What IS that noise?' 'and I could hear this form
breathing at the back door—I mean the sea'
'the sea's the sea' 'throw me the net' 'what's that?'
'That's holes in it to keep it light' 'shhhh'

43

Three cut-out shadows moving on a wall,
a rowing boat pushed like a wooden slipper
over a shelf of shingle . . . two foot down,
it came alive and lifted in the waves.

'Hold steady now!' The two men jumped aboard.
The third, the baker, was knee-deep in water
shoving them slowly out. He felt the hoops
of ice-cold sea contracting on his thighs
and far and wide around him he could hear,
in all that toil of suction and secretion,
the bird-like stones calling under the breakers;
the pied stones and the grey and pigeon stones
and black and round and rolling and knocking
white-throated stones that warble in the wash.
'The sea is full' he said, 'not just of fish
but I can hear the winged souls of the drowned
transforming into pebbles' 'shh—no more.'
'Get in the boat, whip to it, coil the cable;
Candle, you take the oars. As you're a turner
you'll understand these wooden pruned up things.
I'll guide us out. Head for the fishing boats.
There are some dark ones lying big at ease
in the middle water, swinging their prows
as if they grazed their shadows in their sleep.
We want to steer as near them as we dare
to slide above the sandbar to the sea.'

So Candle sculls them slowly from the shallows,
the sea on runners, letting it give and hold
as if his hands are at a factory loom
of miles of silk and moving cylinders;
and he stares up into the stone of his eyes,
he lifts the oars, he feels a bigger darkness,
he yields and feels, controls and strokes and hollows,
carving a sea-form with his arms—a sphere,
a curvilinear figure with two holes.
He rows them out over the long reflections
of window-lights. They go beyond the boatyard,
where metals clank all night. It bangs and dings
as they go rocking for the open sea.
Now he has hitched his heartbeat to the oars.

He rows by breathing, like a mower mows
dreaming a lawn through thirty parallels;
and as they pass the fishing boats, the wind
freshens and blows a circle on their necks
and everywhere the trees, all down the cliffs
are running to them in a shape of waving
like haiku trees, staggering to keep up
the impetus of an extended instant,
and they can hear semi-attentively
and after-differences of sound on sea—
the boom of aeroplanes as they go low
rumbling a bay-wide echo endlessly
and the cuneiform cries of the sea birds
and human voices stopping in mid-air
and under every sound, the lines of water:
'Nunc dimittis Domine' they whisper,
'swish' they whisper 'flutter the boat with wind,
wash it away according to thy word . . .'

'Everything moves' says Candle, 'even Gotham,
even the harbour wall is slowly moving
and if I dip my oar-blade and my oar-blade
there grows another wave between each splash.
How can I row a line consistently
when I can't see, unless I row by spells—
no shape, no place—it is the mastery
of one dark soul over another soul,
this movement of three men over the water.'

The sea is high. They have climbed a black wave
into another world of three steps long
and overboard and only one step wide.
On either side of them a curve. They pause.
They feel it like a tremor in a window
flicker across itself and drop away
and then they slide into the roller vallies
and wavetops crash on them like rotten trees.
The baker bails, the candlemaker rows,
the butcher almost pukes to have the sea
spinning beneath him into scimitars:
the hissing noises as it cuts and meets
and murmurs and the world goes flat again;

and then the thousand epileptic patterns,
the flowers, the momentary islamic marks
which the wind makes on water, all the flash
and twirl and slap and rivalry of waves
mount into aspects of a nothingness
which strives to hold, to make itself by moving.

And then that other sea—the sky. Dark clouds,
the images of waves, were breaking,
falling towards their water-selves as rain;
and in the thick of it, the moon
opened a golden eyelid and looked down,
looked once, looked twice and closed. 'There is no moon.
The moon's gone out' said Butcher, 'this is rain.'
'They say,' said Baker, 'if you oil the moon,
the night goes twice as fast as if you don't.'

The waves that night were everything by turns.
Sometimes they had to shout above the blows
to make themselves be heard and sometimes whispers
competed with the footfall of the oars
and they were rowing in a quiet cathedral.
But it was deafman's buff. The three old men,
they felt as if some power had entered them
and turned their words to foam, they couldn't care
how much they heard, they answered all at once . . .

'What is the moon?' said Candle. 'Is it round?
Do you imagine it an appliqué,
flat like a leaf of gold? Is it so high?'
'The moon is made of water' 'sea is water'
'Somehow the water isn't yet the sea—
it is wave on wave a body struggling
under construction to be something else'
'and the full moon is held in the sea's mind
as her spiritual end' 'the moon is light'
'the sea is light' 'the sea seeks to be round
as if her tides could make a moon by rolling'
'mare imbrium' 'mare nubium'
'mare humorum' 'sinus irridum'
'what unifies the sea?' 'the sea's conjunctions'
'it has it sideways up then flat then sideways'

'the sea contains two spirits lifting glass
who pass each other watching the sharp edge'
'it's a controversy!' 'we sound like waves'
'we sound as if the wind has blown us high
and we must roar until we crumble' 'shhh . . .'

The sea had mastered them. They couldn't make
even the simplest sense of what they witnessed:
the moon, the birds, the crooked boat. They moved
far out between absurdity and wonder,
rocking like figures in a nursery rhyme,
the waves like great smooth beasts shoving them on.

How many men? How many miles from Gotham?
How many fish, feet, hands? They couldn't count.
They only knew the waves were twice as high
and twice as endless as they wished and each
stroke of the oar, each splash, the green-souled waves
came cold alive with pricks of phosphorus
and whispered messages of random numbers:
'Three men, three men of Gotham in a bowl,
the man of Gotham in the moon, the sea,
the six or seven common brittle stars,
and one was blind and two was terrified,
meganyctophanes, four men of Gotham
was hard to balance in the bowl, the moon,
it wasn't even safe to raise a finger
to make a tally of the crew but always
three men three men of Gotham in the moan,
the velvet swimming crab, the file, the flatworm . . .'

And this is why such arguments arose
as to the numbers. They were so confused—
it was like standing in an ancient circle
counting the broken stones, or in a dream
counting your hands and finding three—or four—
that as it happened, each of them in turn
counted the others and forgot himself:
'that's one, that's two of us—so where's the third?'
'I can't see anything' 'has someone gone?'
'listen, who's missing?' 'do it with your eyes,

in ones and starting with the first' 'one two'
'halibu crackibu' 'and who's to say
whether or not the laws of quantities
apply at sea where everything is moving?'
'things disappear' 'the minute we relax
the waves have washed them from the boat' 'and now?'
'I don't know who's not here, but let the rower
starboard about and head for home in silence.'

No one did anything. The candlemaker
was too afraid to turn. He kept on rowing
and muttering to the music of the oars:
'You say there's two of us. You say I'm blind.
I'm frightened. There's no end to where we are.
People have sunk here. It isn't water,
it's fear of light, the proof of sea is fear.
And I can see myself caught in this fear,
rowing a boat of ghosts—you see I can see—
I can see four of us, I heard a man
beating the flocks of horrid barking waves
towards this boat and now he's in with us . . .
there I can feel us: one and two and three
and four of us—we've got an extra man . . .'

Imagine this cold moment: here's the butcher
trying to wipe the error from his eyes;
and here's the baker, counting on his fingers,
his tongue thick, his lips like fluttering eyelids;
the candlemaker with his chin uptilted
tracing a circle in the air; the wind
dead as a doornail. And the fourth person,
now dim, now clear—all they can see of him
is something breathing in the bows, the waves
shaking their wings like summoners behind him—
he makes a movement in the dark, the tshh
of someone moving forward in wet clothes.
The balance alters in the boat. He says:

'I am Old Care   it is my freezing round
to work these seas   many miles out and in
I walk swim fly   half like an oystercatcher
the shaky water under me   always

my feet wet, the ridges blue on my hands
I must make shift even in snow   the cliffs
the webs and cloths of frozen waterfalls
after the cold month when I have fallen
headlong frozen in mid-air   they give way
and spring comes the seathrift comes the gorse comes
the summer birds the sickle path of shoals
comes up the coast and little fishing boats
move out and out for mackerel bright as knives
this is my task   I have to turn seafarers
to water by despair   I call to them
with a mad bird cry   nami no tsuzumi
look at the endlessness   the sea yellow
a level fetch of low saltwater waves
wears them away and it is I—Old Care
sits on the boatside silent without meaning.
I take hope out   I lift the very pearl
out of the dark eye-pupil while it's looking
on waves and waterpatterns   and I dive
I half take off I leave him suddenly
whoever I go haunting   staring down
a metre from the edge   and this is all
only the weather like a painted ball
thrown round and round and round him till he dies'

There were three men of Gotham in a boat,
almost in tears, without a thing to think
but shhh and that was endless, staring down
a metre from the edge of mind. The wind
had blown them wide with nothing to defend
except a little wavy line of seagulls,
tucked in the leeside of the gunwhales, drifting
and paddling back, with feathers soft and lifting.
'What reason do we' shhh—there was this boat
which held them like a rotten half potato;
they could have rolled it over on its side
and swum for heaven, but they sat as tight
as if they'd anchored on the interface
between two wastelands—life and fear of life.

The moon appeared, washed lovelier by rain.
The men three-quarters turned, they quarter-turned,
they tipped their faces broadside to the moon.
The moon appeared and disappeared, appeared
and disappeared and then appeared appeared.
The boat was light with reference to the moon
as if the two connected, but each one
was moving half in touch and half in shadow
and every face was different and alone;
and in the spin of moonshine, there were clouds
flying in zones like zodiacal creatures,
but without pace because the wind had gone.
The sea was miles and miles of palish tin
and a small countermoon was floating there,
very clear, very irregular perfect—
an aspirin in the middle of the world

and may the mystery move them now—the sea
cannot be finished with; each layer is layed
co-terminous with light but more than light
and seamless and invisible in water—
cannot be closed or opened, only entered . . .

'Don't speak' said Butcher, 'quickly, steer us round
the weather side, until your hair blows forward,
then quiet the boat.' The baker took an oar,
the candlemaker shuffled to the bows,
the butcher hugged the net and hoiked it out
in corkscrews from the hold. It was quite wet.
He draped it on the thwarts. The baker slewed
a figure of an eight with the spare oar,
which brought them to the luff side of the moon.
'O moon' said Candle, 'be extraordinary'
'be caught' said Butcher, 'prove that we were wise
to come so far—please—save us from the sea.'
'Amen' said Baker and they threw the net.
They steered away, they pulled the running cord,
the net turned over like a purse, it rose
into the moon and through the moon and out;
the moon broke up in pieces and came whole.
Three times they cast the driftnet, drew it up
and saw the moon dismantle, saw the net

grope for a ghost and gather what it could
and ropes of water reeve themselves away.
Three times the moon was shattered like a bowl
and slowly mended by the moon.

                     The moon
was in another world, the moon was flying
amazed around a floating point, the sea
was upside down in air and touching nothing
and without purpose there was fluke and balance
of light on water moving across water,
which broke in pieces and came whole again.

'Is it alive?' said Candle, 'Can I feel?
Have you gone quiet with the weight of it
or cold or what? Or is it what I thought—
that we're the prisoners—that the moon herself
has caught us in a net; if we step out
over the border of our wooden bowl,
I know what world there is, what huge sea-light
binds us, winds like a chain through everything . . .'

No sound, only the knocking of the boatwood,
the net clacking its floats; until the darkness,
in living moments like a bud, gives way
to paler clouds, the almost apple green
and ice blue lines increase above the sea
and squares of water, pink and pea-leaf green
catch fire as if the sea became a star;
and after that, as I came down through Gotham,
that light which the horizons of all seas
imply beyond—a kind of agitated
surreal and weightless curve—I saw it move
to close the space above a tiny boat
and in that boat, I thought I saw three men
and one was standing like a cormorant
who dries his wings; the spinning of the earth,
the wind, the sun were pulling them away.
I heart their voices on the waves: 'Look up'
'what's that?' 'it's water' 'it's the moon' 'how far?'
'how many miles is it?' if we go on
beyond the crack of the horizon, wind

has broken down the moon. Silver in handfuls
and leaf of fold are floating on the sea'
'how shall we carry it?' 'we've got a bowl,
but it's a sea that may go on some time—
give me the left oar, Baker—close your eyes
and when the journey ends, I'll give a shout.'

OXFORD POETS

Fleur Adcock

Moniza Alvi

Kamau Brathwaite

Joseph Brodsky

Basil Bunting

Daniela Crăsnaru

Michael Donaghy

Keith Douglas

D. J. Enright

Roy Fisher

Ida Affleck Graves

Ivor Gurney

David Harsent

Gwen Harwood

Anthony Hecht

Zbigniew Herbert

Thomas Kinsella

Brad Leithauser

Derek Mahon

Jamie McKendrick

Sean O'Brien

Alice Oswald

Peter Porter

Craig Raine

Zsuzsa Rakovszky

Henry Reed

Christopher Reid

Stephen Romer

Carole Satyamurti

Peter Scupham

Jo Shapcott

Penelope Shuttle

Anne Stevenson

George Szirtes

Grete Tartler

Edward Thomas

Charles Tomlinson

Marina Tsvetaeva

Chris Wallace-Crabbe

Hugo Williams